Twenty to Ma...

Tags & Toppers

Michelle Powell

Search Press

First published in Great Britain 2008

Search Press Limited
Wellwood, North Farm Road,
Tunbridge Wells, Kent TN2 3DR

Text copyright © Michelle Powell 2008

Photographs by Debbie Patterson,
Search Press Studios

Photographs and design copyright
© Search Press Ltd 2008

ISBN: 978-1-84448-337-2

Printed in Malaysia.

Suppliers
If you have difficulty in obtaining any of the
materials and equipment mentioned in this
book, then please visit the Search Press website
for details of suppliers: www.searchpress.com

Dedication
This book is for Paul, Sue,
Hayley and Rikki Smith,
with love.

Contents

Introduction

Tags and toppers are basically mini, three-dimensional sticker motifs made using pretty papers, glitter and ribbons that are designed to adorn your crafting creations, cards and scrapbook pages. Craft shops are filled to overflowing with gorgeously themed packs of toppers and tags, but it is so easy and so much fun to make your own that I often wonder who buys them, despite the lure of the pretty packaging!

This book shows you how, with a little imagination, you can create toppers and tags using basic craft materials and tools, and for a fraction of the cost of shop-bought items. If you have cutting machines, punches and dies these will speed up your topper making, but a simple craft knife or scissors will work just as well. Best of all, these toppers need such small pieces of paper and ribbon that they are ideal for using up all the leftover scraps from other projects.

So next time you are tempted to buy a pack of toppers, go for the craft punches, ribbons and pretty papers instead and enjoy the creative process of crafting your own tag and topper designs and the satisfaction of knowing you made them.

Templates

Glitter Fish (pages 8–9)

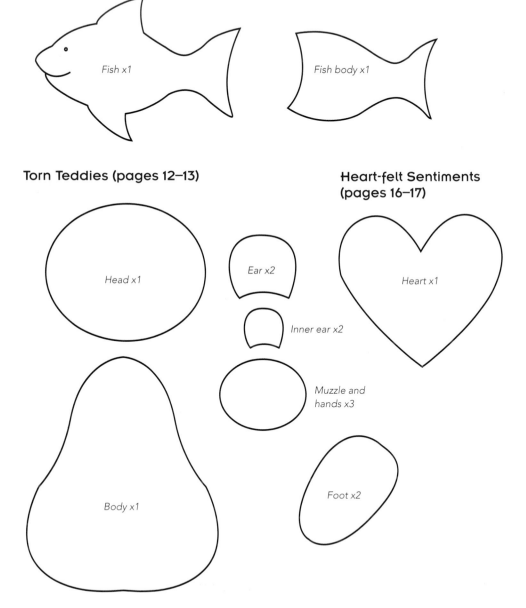

Fish x1

Fish body x1

Torn Teddies (pages 12–13)

Heart-felt Sentiments (pages 16–17)

Head x1

Ear x2

Inner ear x2

Muzzle and hands x3

Heart x1

Body x1

Foot x2

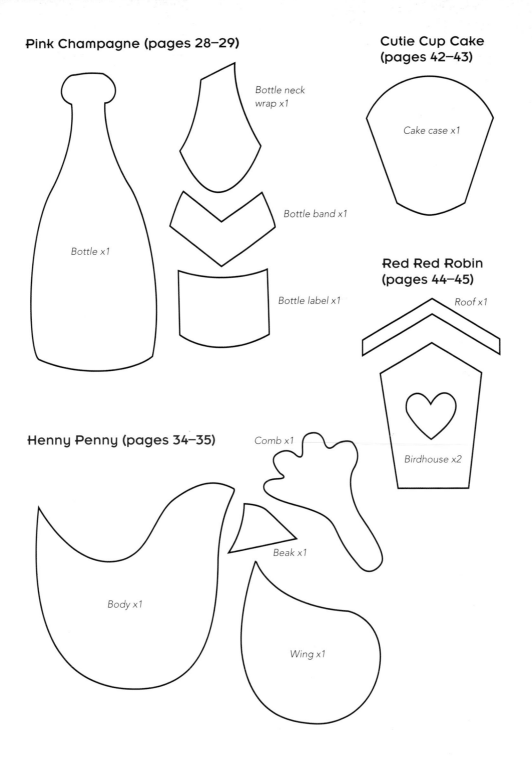

Pink Champagne (pages 28–29)

Bottle neck wrap x1

Bottle band x1

Bottle label x1

Bottle x1

Cutie Cup Cake (pages 42–43)

Cake case x1

Red Red Robin (pages 44–45)

Roof x1

Birdhouse x2

Henny Penny (pages 34–35)

Comb x1

Beak x1

Body x1

Wing x1

Glitter Fish

Materials:

Coloured card
Glitter card
Thin ribbon
Chalks
Glitter
Self-adhesive gemstones

Tools:

Small flower punch
Tiny hole punch
Die-cutting machine and
   embossing folder
Glue pen
All-purpose glue
3D foam pads

Variation

Make a similar fish with stripes of glitter rather than the gemstones. Stick to the top of a long strip of card and add a ribbon to create a bookmark.

Instructions:

1 Using the templates given on page 6, cut the fish and fish body shapes from coloured and glitter card respectively.

2 Chalk the edges of the fish shape and cut short fringing on the tail and fins. Punch a tiny hole for the eye, cut a slit for the mouth and chalk on a cheek.

3 Glue the glitter fish body to the fish shape. Stick on five gemstones and add a line of glitter.

4 Cut a rectangle of card 3.5 x 5.5cm (1½ x 2¼in) and emboss it using an embossing folder in a die-cutting machine. Alternatively use ready-embossed card.

5 Mount it on a slightly larger card rectangle. Wrap the lower part with ribbon and knot.

6 Punch a small circle and flower shape and add a gemstone. Glue it on to the topper. Add the fish to the topper using a 3D foam pad.

Fishy Fun

Fish are such a fantastic subject for crafting as they come in all sorts of colour combinations and patterns. Go to town and create sparkly fish in shades of pink and purple for a dazzling design.

Glitzy Girl

Materials:

Card handbag shape
Thin organza ribbon
Glitter card
Mirror card
Brad
Self-adhesive gemstones

Tools:

Flower punch
Leaf-sprig punch
Perforating tool
All-purpose glue
3D foam pads

Variation

Create a simpler bag with a cord handle and decorate a shoe shape. Mount on matted squares as before and use them to decorate a greetings card.

Instructions:

1 Fold the handbag shape and add perforated lines to look like stitches.

2 Glue thin ribbon around the lower part of the bag front and add three tiny gemstones.

3 Add a brad to the bag flap and stick the bag closed using a 3D foam pad.

4 Punch two flower shapes from glitter card. Curl the petals and layer. Place a gemstone in the centre.

5 Punch two leaf-sprig shapes from mirror card. Glue the leaves and flower in place on the bag.

6 Cut a 4cm (1½in) square of mirror card and mount it on a 4.5cm (1¾in) square of glitter card using 3D foam pads. Attach the bag to the mount using a single 3D foam pad.

Glamour Girl

For a more sophisticated look, change the colours used to a glamorous gold and black. Also try black and white or red and black for striking effects.

Torn Teddies

Materials:

Coloured card
Organza ribbon
Chalks

Tools:

Tiny hole punch
Small circle punch
Die-cutting machine and
   embossing folder
All-purpose glue
3D foam pads

Variation

*Decorate a tag with a torn teddy. Make
the head in the same way and tear a
larger semi-circle for the body. Add a
knot of ribbon for a bow tie.*

Instructions:

1 Trace and transfer the templates given on page 6 on to the back of coloured card.

2 Tear out each piece in turn, tearing away from you so that the front of the card has a nice torn edge.

3 Chalk the edges of each piece and chalk on the cheeks. Punch tiny holes for eyes.

4 Punch a small circle and cut it in quarters, using one to make a nose. Stick in place using a 3D foam pad and add a pencil line to the muzzle.

5 Cut a 3.5cm (1½in) square of card and emboss it using an embossing folder in a die-cutting machine. Alternatively use ready-embossed or patterned card.

6 Wrap the square with ribbon and knot at the top. Assemble the teddy using 3D foam pads for dimension.

Pretty Panda

This teddy design is so easy to transform into a cute panda. Use a black and white colour scheme and add two small, torn kidney shapes for the black panda eyes. Add a punched blossom to complete the transformation!

Daisy Daisy

Materials:

Coloured card
Glitter card
Ribbon
Kebab sticks
Paint
Small tin
Shredded tissue paper
Oasis

Tools:

Large daisy punch
Circle punches
Small flower punch
Tiny hole punch
Paintbrush
All-purpose glue
3D foam pads

Variation

Make just one flower with a centre, omitting the kebab stick. Attach this to a square of card, mounted on a tag shape. Alternatively, use this daisy topper for a bold, floral card.

Instructions:

1 Punch or hand cut four daisy shapes, six 2.5cm (1in) circles, two small flowers and two small circles from coloured or glitter card.

2 Punch tiny holes in two of the 2.5cm (1in) circles and glue each to a different-coloured 2.5cm (1in) circle.

3 Layer the small flowers and circles on the remaining two 2.5cm (1in) circles and use 3D foam pads to assemble.

4 Paint three kebab sticks green, leave to dry and cut to 18cm (7in), 15cm (6in) and 12cm (4¾in) lengths.

5 Using two layers of 3D foam pads, attach a flower centre to the end of each kebab stick, and then stick this to the daisy shape.

6 Cover a small tin with coloured card. Tie a bow of ribbon around and add the remaining flower and centre using 3D foam pads.

7 Fill the tin with oasis, using the tin to cut the shape. Top with shredded paper and push in the flowers.

Fantasy Flowers
Use plenty of artistic licence to vary your daisy colours to shades of rose pink, wine and cream for a more classical look. Team with a brown tin and stripy ribbon for a modern 'home décor' style.

Heart-felt Sentiments

Materials:

Coloured card

Organza ribbon

Glitter

Self-adhesive gemstones

Tools:

Scalloped square punch

Hole punch

Die-cutting machine and
   embossing folder

Glue pen

3D foam pads

Variation
*Stick an embossed and glittered
heart on a rectangular mount. Mat
on mirror card and add to the front
of a greetings card.*

Instructions:

1 Cut the heart shape using the template given on page 6 from coloured card. Punch a hole in the centre of the heart.

2 Emboss the heart using an embossing folder in a die-cutting machine. Alternatively, use ready-embossed card or hand emboss using a stencil.

3 Outline the heart using a glue pen and sprinkle with glitter. Stick on two gemstones.

4 Punch a scalloped square shape and tie the ribbon around the square, threading both ends through the hole in the heart. Knot and trim the ribbon ends.

Love Heart

For a soft, pretty look, vary the colours used to silver and pastel pinks. Combine with silver gift boxes for favours and tables decorated with rose petals for a really romantic wedding theme.

Easter Bunny

Materials:
Coloured card
Narrow ribbon
Chalks
Black pen
Glitter

Tools:
Heart punch
Large daisy punch
Small circle punch
Corner-rounding punch
Scallop scissors
Die-cutting machine and
    embossing folder
Glue pen
All-purpose glue
3D foam pads

Variation
Omit the egg and hand cut a large carrot shape. Add a strip of card fringed on both sides for the carrot top. Mount on a scalloped circle and use this topper to decorate a mini basket of Easter eggs.

Instructions:

1 Punch or cut a heart shape from coloured card. Place it so that the left lobe of the heart is at the top to form a head, and fold the right lobe in towards the centre to create a folded arm.

2 Punch a daisy shape and trim off two petals. Bend them to make the ears and attach to the back of the head using a 3D foam pad.

3 Cut a small oval shape and attach it to the front of the face to form a muzzle. Add a quarter circle nose.

4 Chalk the edges of each piece and add chalked cheeks. Draw on black dots for the eyes.

5 Hand cut an egg shape, chalk the edges and add glitter dots.

6 Cut a strip of card using scallop scissors and attach as a band around the egg. Tie a piece of narrow ribbon around the egg.

7 Cut a rectangle 5.5 x 3.5cm (2¼ x 1½in) and emboss in a die-cutting machine. Round the corners and attach the bunny and egg to the topper.

Pink Rabbit

Make a white bunny with pink chalking and add a purple glittered egg for a younger, fun variation on the colour theme.

Flutter-by Butterfly

Materials:

Coloured card
Glitter card
Wire
Chalks
Glitter
Self-adhesive gemstones

Tools:

Heart punch
Large daisy punch
Small circle punch
Scalloped square punch
Wire cutter
Glue pen
All-purpose glue
3D foam pads

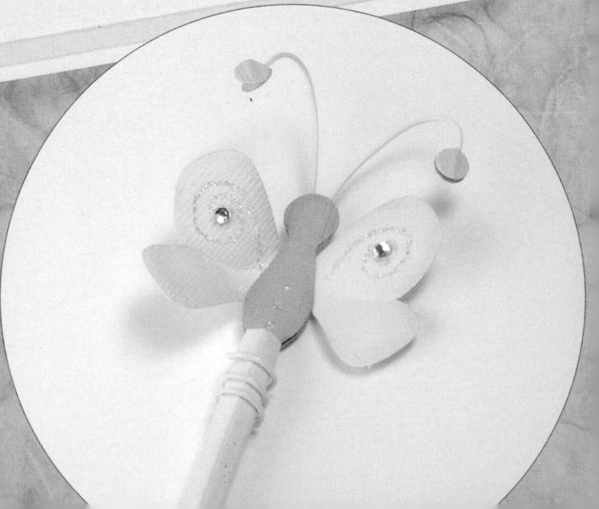

Variation

Omit the square mount and wrap the trailing wire around a pencil to create a pencil topper.

Instructions:

1 Punch two heart shapes, one daisy shape and four circles from coloured card.

2 Chalk the edges of each piece.

3 Trim two of the petals from the daisy shape to create two body pieces, trimming the base of each petal in a circular shape to create the head.

4 Cut 8cm (3¼in) of wire and glue two circles to each end. Bend in half. Stick to the back of one of the body pieces to create the antennae.

5 Cut 9cm (3½in) of wire and glue one end to the base of the same body piece. Glue the wings in place. Glue the second body piece on top.

6 Bend the trailing wire and mount on a punched scalloped square of glitter card, matted on a slightly larger card square.

7 Decorate the wings with glitter and gemstones.

Back to Nature

Create a colour variation using natural muted shades of orange and sage green. Punch holes in the wings for a rustic alternative to glitter and gemstone decorations.

Smiley Snowman

Materials:
Coloured card

Tools:
Oval punch
Tiny, small, medium and large circle punches
Small hole punch
Die-cutting machine and holly-leaf die
All-purpose glue
3D foam pads

For this Christmas decoration place the topper inside a plastic bauble and fill behind with chocolate coins. Add a ribbon hanging loop.

Variations
Mount a snowman head topper on scalloped and regular squares of card for a gift box decoration, or add a hand-cut scarf and hat to the head for a snowman tag design.

22

Instructions:

1 Punch or cut an oval 5 x 3cm (2 x 1¼in) for the head. Punch a small 1.2cm (½in) circle for the cheek and glue it in place.

2 Cut a smile into the head and punch two tiny holes for the eyes. Hand cut a carrot nose and stick it to the head using a 3D foam pad.

3 Use a die cutter to cut two holly leaves, and a small hole punch to cut a berry.

4 Punch or cut two large 7.5cm (3in) circles, one for the body and one for the backing.

5 Glue the body circle offset on to the backing circle, turn it over and trim off the excess body.

6 Assemble the snowman head using 3D foam pads and stick it to the body.

Frosty the Snowman
Use cool, contemporary colours of blue and lavender, and combine with glitter card for a frosty look. Use lime green holly leaves with a pink berry to complete the look.

Button Bloom

Materials:

Coloured card
Patterned papers
Leather flower shape
Large button
Ribbon
Thick card
Chalk
Black inkpad

Tools:

Double-sided tape
All-purpose glue

Variation

Cut a square of card and mount on a slightly larger, patterned paper square. Stick to a candle votive. Tie on a small leather flower, wrapping the ribbon around the votive candle and knotting in the middle of the flower.

Instructions:

1 Cut a rectangle of thick card 11 x 3.5cm (4¼ x 1½in). Cover with coloured card.

2 Tear two pieces of patterned paper about 3cm (1¼in) wide and stick across the centre of the card using double-sided tape.

3 Turn over and trim off the excess. Chalk and ink the edges. Leave to dry.

4 Cut 11cm (4¼in) of ribbon and thread the button on to the flower shape. Tie the ribbon in a knot on the front and trim the ends.

5 Glue the flower to the card rectangle.

Pretty in Pink
Use a pink flower shape and button teamed with chocolate brown for a really trendy colour scheme that is perfect for home interiors.

Topiary Topper

Materials:
Coloured card
Chalks
Glitter
Self-adhesive gemstone

Tools:
Flowerpot punch
Small flower punch
Deckle-edge scissors
Glue pen
All-purpose glue
3D foam pads

Variation
Create a pot-plant topper with a teardrop-shaped tree covered in punched flowers. Mount on a tag shape and add a ribbon bow.

26

Instructions:

1 Tear a rectangle of coloured card 5.5 x 3cm (2¼ x 1¼in) and screw it up tightly. Flatten it back out.

2 Mount the torn rectangle on a card rectangle 6.5 x 4cm (2½ x 1½in) using 3D foam pads.

3 Draw a 3cm (1¼in) circle on the back of coloured card and cut it out using deckle-edge scissors. This will form the top of the tree.

4 Chalk the edges of the tree and add dots of glitter.

5 Punch or hand cut two flowerpot shapes, chalk and cut just the rim off one. Mount the rim on the pot using a 3D foam pad.

6 Hand cut a tree trunk 3mm (⅛in) wide and 3cm (1¼in) long. Assemble the tree and pot using 3D foam pads on the rectangle.

7 Punch a small flower shape, bend the petals up and add a gemstone centre. Glue to the side of the pot.

Lime Trees
Use brighter shades of lime and turquoise together with an orange pot for a funky variation.

Pink Champagne

Materials:

Coloured card
Mirror card
Cord
Narrow ribbon
Wire
Die-cut or sticker numbers
Eyelet
Chalks
Glitter

Tools:

Small tag punch
Pointy flower punch
Hole punch
Circle punch
Eyelet punch and setter
Wire cutter and round-
  nosed pliers
All-purpose glue
Double-sided punch tape
Glue pen
3D foam pads

Variation

Decorate a greetings card with a bottle topper and mount on a rectangle of card decorated with dots of glitter. Add gemstones and a round tag tied to the card with a length of stretchy cord.

Instructions:

1 Cut the bottle, neck wrap, label and band shapes using the templates given on page 7 from coloured and mirror card as appropriate.

2 Chalk the edges of the bottle shape and add a line of glitter down one side using the glue pen.

3 Assemble the bottle using 3D foam pads for dimension. Add a punched circle to the band.

4 Cut 20cm (7¾in) of wire, fold at 7cm (2¾in) and bend each end into a spiral. Stick the wire to the back of the bottle neck using a 3D foam pad.

5 Punch or cut a small tag shape. Set with an eyelet and add number stickers or die cuts. Tie to the neck of the bottle using narrow ribbon.

6 Cut a tag shape 10 x 4.5cm (4 x 1¾in) and chalk the edges. Punch pointy flower shapes from double-sided punch tape and stick them to the tag. Add glitter.

7 Assemble the tag sticking the bottle in place. Punch a hole in the top and add the cord.

Champagne Fizz
Revert to traditional champagne bottle colours of gold and bottle green for more masculine appeal. Also try a black bottle and silver label for a more sophisticated look.

Winter Wishes

Materials:
Coloured card
Dotty mesh
Mini bulldog clip
Spiral clip
Self-adhesive gemstone
Chalks
Glitter

Tools:
Snowflake die cutter
All-purpose glue
Narrow double-sided tape
Small 3D foam pads

Variation
*Make a square version of the
snowflake topper and attach
to a small gift tag.*

Instructions:

1 Use a die cutter to cut and assemble a snowflake shape from coloured card. Add a gemstone to the centre.

2 Cut a 3cm (1¼in) square of card and chalk the edges. Mount the snowflake in the centre using small 3D foam pads.

3 Cut a 7.5 x 5cm (3 x 2in) rectangle of card and chalk the edges.

4 Add a line of narrow double-sided tape to the lower edge of the rectangle and sprinkle with glitter.

5 Cut a 7.5 x 5cm (3 x 2in) rectangle of dotty mesh and clip it at an angle to the card rectangle using both the spiral and mini bulldog clips.

6 Use 3D foam pads to attach the snowflake square to the mesh rectangle.

Frosty Flakes

For a really cool wintry look, choose icy shades of turquoise on which to mount the snowflake. Cut the snowflake from bright white card rather than the cream card used for the more rustic brown and olive colour scheme.

Retro Chic

Materials:

Coloured card
Mirror card
Patterned paper
Brad

Tools:

Personal cutter and cartridge
Circle punch
Corner-rounding punch
Double-sided tape
3D foam pads

Variation

Make a square rimmed-style tag with rounded corners by cutting a mirror card rim. Thread a length of ribbon through the top and fix with a brad.

Instructions:

1 Use a personal cutter to cut a flower shape from coloured card. Alternatively hand cut or punch the flower.

2 Punch a circle for the flower centre and attach it to the flower using a brad.

3 Cut a 4.5cm (1¾in) square of coloured card and stick a strip of torn patterned paper 2.5cm (1in) wide along the bottom. Round the corners.

4 Cut a 5.5cm (2¼in) square of mirror card, round the corners and mount the flower and coloured card square on top using 3D foam pads.

Flower Power

Bright orange and a lime and purple striped paper create a 1970s' 'flower power' look for this topper and tag.

Henny Penny

Materials:
Coloured card
Small-print fabrics
Button
Hessian
White pen

Tools:
Small and medium hole punches
Pinking shears
Wide double-sided tape
All-purpose glue
3D foam pads

Variation
Make a hen topper and cut two body shapes. Sandwich a kebab stick between them and tie with a strip of hessian to make a rustic plant poke.

Instructions:

1 Stick some wide double-sided tape to coloured card and attach a section of each of the fabrics.

2 Transfer the templates given on page 7 to the back of the corresponding fabric-covered card pieces and cut out.

3 Assemble the hen using all-purpose glue and 3D foam pads for the wings.

4 Cut a 2cm (¾in) square of fabric using pinking shears for the patch and stick it in place with a 3D foam pad. Add a button to the top.

5 Punch a small circle for the eye and a medium circle for the cheek and glue in place. Add a tiny dot of white pen to the eye. Mount on a 7 x 5.5cm (2¾ x 2¼in) rectangle of hessian.

Mother Hen

Banish the rustic country cottage feel with this totally pantomime version of the hen in a pink, lime and lavender colour scheme. Leave off the comb and wattle to create Mother Goose!

35

Felt Flowers

Materials:
Coloured felt
Embroidery thread
Button

Tools:
Pinking shears
Needle
All-purpose glue

Variation

Cut 22cm (8¾in) of cord and loop it through a key ring. Glue the flower to one end of the cord and two leaves to the other to create a key ring.

Instructions:

1 Use pinking shears to cut out two circles of coloured felt, 4cm (1½in) and 5cm (2in) in diameter. Cut into each circle in eight places to make petals.

2 Use regular scissors to cut out a leaf shape and a small circle 2.5cm (1in) in diameter.

3 Stitch one long stitch down the centre of each petal, layer all three circles with the button on top and stitch together.

4 Stitch veins on to the leaf and stitch the leaf to the back of the flower.

5 Cut a 5.5cm (2¼in) square of felt and stitch a blanket stitch around the outside edge. Glue the flower in the centre of the square.

Cool Colours
Use super cool shades of blue, yellow, lime and turquoise felt combined with matching thread stitches to make extra funky felt flower toppers.

Figgy Pudding

Materials:

Coloured card
Glitter
Ribbon

Tools:

Small, medium and large
  circle punches

Scalloped circle punch

Hole punch

Die-cutting machine and
  holly-leaf die

Glue pen

3D foam pads

Variation

*Make a hanging Christmas
decoration. Make two pudding
tags and a third with a snowflake
replacing the sauce and holly.
Thread them together using
ribbon and back each with
another 6.5cm (2½in) circle.*

Instructions:

1 Punch or cut circles 6.5cm (2½in) in diameter for the backing and 4cm (1½in) in diameter for the pudding. Also punch or cut a 5.5cm (2¼in) scalloped circle.

2 Punch another 4cm (1½in) circle from pale card for the sauce. Cut it roughly in half with a very wavy line.

3 Add dots of glitter to the pudding and stick the sauce in place using 3D foam pads. Stick this to the circle mounts using 3D foam pads.

4 Die cut two holly leaves and punch a berry. Add to the pudding using 3D foam pads.

5 Punch a hole in the top of the tag and add a length of ribbon.

The Christmas pudding is such an iconic symbol you can create it in any shade and it is still obvious what it is. This pink pudding has silver holly and a mauve mount and yet still looks every bit as Christmassy as the traditional version.

Love Letters

Materials:
Coloured card
Heart-shaped buttons
Writing paper
Envelope

Tools:
Perforating tool
Circle punch
Double-sided tape
All-purpose glue

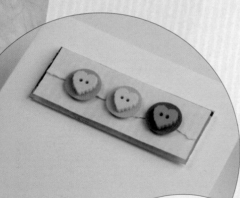

Variations
Mount three tiny toppers on a rectangle of torn paper and mat with mirror card, or create a tiny tag for a postage stamp box.

Instructions:

1 Punch or cut four 1.2cm (½in) diameter circles from coloured card.

2 Glue a heart-shaped button to each circle in a contrasting colour.

3 Tear a 1.5cm (¾in) strip from a piece of writing paper and stick it along the top of another piece using double-sided tape.

4 Perforate along the tear line using a perforating tool, then bend up the torn edge slightly.

5 Perforate three lines across the flap of the envelope. Glue three heart toppers to the paper and one to the envelope along the perforated lines.

Pretty Pastels
This simple design will work in any colour scheme such as the pinks and blues shown here. It could also look stunning in gold and black or shades of white. Purchase your buttons first and match your papers to them.

Cutie Cup Cake

Materials:
Coloured card
Glitter card
Striped card
Self-adhesive gemstone
Chalks
Glitter

Tools:
Scallop scissors
Circle punch
Small leaf punch
Small daisy punch
All-purpose glue
Glue pen
3D foam pads

Variation
Mount the cake topper on a circular backing piece decorated with dots of glitter and add the topper to the front of a small gift bag. Add a small punched tag decorated with a flower to the bag handle.

Instructions:

1 Punch a 4cm (1½in) diameter circle from glitter card and trim off the lower edge in an arc shape using scallop scissors.

2 Transfer the template given on page 7 to the back of the striped card and cut out. Alternatively punch a 4cm (1½in) diameter circle from striped card and trim about 5mm (¼in) from each side diagonally to create a cake-case shape.

3 Cut a rectangle of card 3.5cm x 8mm (1½ x ½in) for the candle and chalk the edges. Punch or cut a small leaf shape for the flame. Add a tiny line of glitter.

4 Stick the icing to the cake case using 3D foam pads. Glue the candle to the back of the icing and stick the flame on top.

5 Punch a small daisy shape. Add glitter to the petals and a gemstone to the centre. Curl the petals and stick the flower in place on the cake.

Chocolate Heaven

Use yummy shades of chocolate brown, pistachio and duck egg blue to make a more grown-up version of the cup-cake topper.

43

Red Red Robin

Materials:
Coloured card
Chequered paper
Gold pen
Chalks
Black pen

Tools:
Leaf punch
Heart punch
Egg-shape punch
Double-sided tape
3D foam pads

Variation
Make a birdhouse without a stand and add the bird to the house front. Mount on a circle of card with torn paper along the bottom.

Instructions:

1 Punch or cut a leaf shape and an egg shape. Trim the leaf stalk into a beak shape and colour it in with gold pen.

2 Add chalk to the bird's breast, cheek and wing. Stick the wing in place using a 3D foam pad and draw on an eye.

3 Cut two birdhouses and one roof shape using the templates given on page 7. Punch a heart-shaped hole in one house shape and chalk the centre of the other.

4 Cut a strip of card 5mm (¼in) wide and cut it into 4.5cm (1¾in) and 2.5cm (1in) lengths. Assemble the birdhouse using 3D foam pads.

5 Cut a rectangle of card 10 x 4cm (4 x 1½in) and mount it on another rectangle 10.5 x 4.5cm (4¼ x 1¾in).

6 Tear a piece of patterned paper 3cm (1¼in) wide and glue it to the bottom of the smaller rectangle. Use 3D foam pads to attach the bird and birdhouse to the backing rectangle. Draw on the bird's legs.

Birdie House
By simply changing the colours of this topper design you can create a card for any occasion. Use springtime shades of lime and yellow to remove the Christmassy feel.

Baby Face

Materials:

Coloured card
Striped paper
White pen
Chalk
Ribbon
Brad

Tools:

Personal cutter and cartridge
Circle punch
Double-sided tape
3D foam pads

Variations

Make an embellishment
for a mini scrapbook.
Mount a baby face on a
5cm (2in) square with the
corners rounded. Add
striped paper to the lower
2cm (¾in) of the square.
Alternatively, add a flower
to a circular mount and
use as decoration for a
party bag of sweets.

Instructions:

1 Use a personal cutter to cut a baby face, bow, hair, tag and flower shapes. Alternatively hand cut or punch the shapes.

2 Add chalk to the edges of each piece and add chalked cheeks. Punch a circle for the flower centre and chalk.

3 Cut a strip of striped paper 5 x 1.5cm (2 x ¾in) and stick it to the bottom of the tag.

4 Draw a broken white line around the edge of the tag and flower centre.

5 Using 3D foam pads assemble the baby face and flower and attach them to the tag.

6 Cut a 10cm (4in) piece of ribbon, fold it in half and attach to the tag using a brad.

Baby's Birthday Party
Cheerful shades of lime, lemon and lavender change these tag and topper designs so that they are suitable for both boys and girls. They are ideal for decorating party bags for a baby's birthday.

Acknowledgements

Many thanks to the talented team at Search Press – Roz, Katie, Debbie and Ellie. Also thanks, as always, to Christian, Mum and Dad for all their help and support along the way.

Publishers' Note

If you would like more books on papercrafts, try the following Search Press titles:

Paper Punching by Michelle Powell, 2007
Iris Folding by Michelle Powell, 2008
Papercrafts for Christmas, 2008
Encyclopedia of Cardmaking Techniques, 2007
Handmade Victorian Cards by Joanna Sheen, 2007
Handmade Art Nouveau Cards by Judy Balchin, 2007